SUNNY AND MALCOLM

Sunny and Malcolm

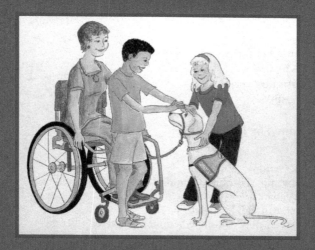

written by
Cynthia Crosson

illustrated by
Carole Williams

Haley's
Athol, Massachusetts

Haley's
488 South Main Street
Athol, MA 01331
haley.antique@verizon.net
800.215.8805

Copy edited by Debra Ellis.

Crosson, Cynthia.
    Sunny and Malcolm / Cynthia Crosson ; illustrated by Carole Williams.
    Athol, MA : Haley's, [2017]
    1. Service dogs--Juvenile fiction. 2. Disabled veterans--Juvenile fiction. 3. Service-disabled veterans--Juvenile fiction. 4. Human-animal communication-- Juvenile fiction. 5. Families--Juvenile fiction. I. Title. II. Williams, Carole.
    ISBN: 978-0-9967730-2-7 (trade paperback)
    ISBN: 978-0-9967730-3-4 (hardcover)
    PZ7.C88285.S86 2017

For Ron, Amanda, Taylor, Austin, and Madison
the real heroes

Contents

We Meet Spark

I never imagined I would meet my best friend through a dog—or at a veterans' center for that matter. Well, the dog wasn't just any dog. He's Spark, my mom's service dog. And the veterans' center is special, too, because that's where my mom is trying to get her life back. I guess I should start from the beginning.

I'm Sunny—short for Sunshine. I know it's a different kind of name, but Mom says she named me that because I was such a happy baby and brought sunshine into her life. I think she and my dad were having a lot of arguments, because when I was three, he left us, and my parents got divorced. I hear from him, but he lives in California and we live on the East Coast, so I don't see him much.

My mom's been a soldier ever since I can remember. My dad was, too. A couple of years ago, Mom got sent to Afghanistan, and I stayed with my Aunt June and Uncle Bob. It wasn't that bad, because Mom talked to me on Skype and through e-mail.

Until one day we got a message that she'd been hurt. That was a pretty scary time. I don't remember too much about those months when she was in an Army hospital back here in the United States. I just remember how scared I was. We went down to visit her, and I found out that she damaged her spine in an explosion, so she can't walk anymore. I couldn't imagine what that would mean to us.

She had to stay in the veterans hospital a while longer while she learned how to do things without being able to walk. Before Mom came home, some people came into our house and built a lot of stuff "to make it easier for her," they told me. She would be in a wheelchair, and they had to take up the wall-to-wall carpeting. They also lowered the counters in the kitchen and bathroom so she could reach them from her wheelchair and even made some doors wider so the chair could get through them. It was kind of strange at first, but I was so excited that Mom was coming home.

Mom was a lot thinner than when she went to Afghanistan, and it was strange seeing her sitting in a wheelchair all the time. And there were things I had to help with that I didn't have to before. But I was almost nine, and I didn't mind. She told me I was a pretty good help.

But then six months later we got Spark, and that made things even better. Mom heard about an organization called Assistance Dogs for Better Living—or ABL—that places specially trained service dogs to help people who need them. There were times when I couldn't be there, and Mom found it hard. She couldn't always reach things she dropped or open some doors or get to the phone quickly. So, Mom applied for a service dog and went for an interview to see if she was accepted. When she told me we were going to get a service dog to help her with some stuff, I was really excited.

"This won't be a family dog," Mom told me. "He'll be my special helper and will go with me everywhere. You'll only be able to play with him when he's not working."

That was okay. We had a dog when I was really little, but that was a long time ago, and I almost remembered cuddling up to her when we both lay on the bed.

Two weeks after her interview Mom got a call that she had been accepted to get a service dog. Then, she went for a two-week training to get her dog while I went back to Aunt June's. I could hardly wait for them to come home.

Mom had a special van with hand controls so she could drive herself. The back door opened and a ramp came down so she could wheel herself into the van. Then she could roll herself up to the front and lock her chair into driving position.

The van was bright red, and I could see it coming a block away. Aunt June and Uncle Bob brought me to our house before Mom arrived home from the training with her dog so I could be there when she got there.

And there was the van, coming up the street. Mom unlocked her wheelchair and rolled down the ramp out of the van. The dog was still inside the van and I kept trying to peek inside to see him.

"Just wait!" Mom laughed. "You'll meet him soon enough."

At her command, a yellow dog jumped out of the van and went right over to her carrying his leash. She took the leash, patted his head, and gave him a treat.

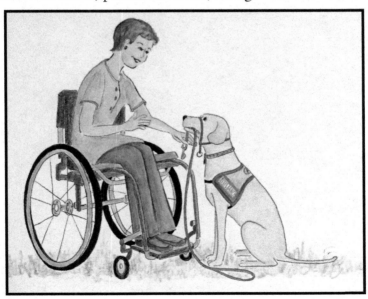

"Now go say hello," Mom told the dog, and he came over to me wagging his tail and looking really happy to see me.

"This is Spark," said Mom.

I had no idea how this dog would change our lives.

Malcolm

Spark could do a lot more than pick up his leash. He opened things and picked up things like Mom's keys. He got her the portable phone when it rang, and he could even open the fridge and get her a bottled drink when she asked him.

"And if I fall, he will bark and let you know that I need help," Mom told us.

"That's a good thing!" said Aunt June. "I worry about you, Amanda."

"Once a big sister, always a big sister," Mom joked. She always teased about how her sister, June, who is ten years older than Mom, tried to take care of her, never more than since she had been hurt.

But Mom was pretty independent and learning quickly what she could do and when she needed to ask for help.

"I think this big guy will be a lot of help," Mom said as she stroked Spark's head. He looked pleased.

Spark not only helps Mom. I think he has made her feel better, too. She was pretty unhappy when she first came home from the hospital after she was hurt, although she tried not to let me know. Her therapist suggested that she apply for a service dog and that's how we got Spark. Once Spark was around, though, she really seemed happy. We'd walk him together and play catch with him in the

back yard or at Silver Park near our house. Mom got out a lot more and seemed more like her old self. She came to my school events and softball games, and everyone made a big deal over Spark. He seemed to appreciate their attention, but he always looked to Mom to tell him what to do. I knew he was my mom's special dog, but I loved having him in the family.

I also knew there were still things that bothered Mom about her time in Afghanistan. When she first came home, she had terrible nightmares, and her crying often woke me up. That situation got better with Spark, though, as he seemed to be a comfort to her when she had bad dreams. But one day she told me she was going to a veteran's center where they worked with veterans who needed help dealing with what they had experienced. She told me she would have her own therapist. She also said there might be times when I could come in and talk about my feelings, too. I figured I didn't really need that, but if it would make Mom happy, I'd go.

Mom seemed to enjoy going to the vet center, as she called it. I think she liked talking with other people who understood what had happened to her. She went while I was in school, but she told me about it when I got home. They had activities and social events that she said were fun. She told me that Spark was a big hit, too. He greeted everyone when she told him he could, and she was really proud of how well-behaved and well-trained he was. Mom's counselor said there used to be another veteran who had a service dog, but he moved away. The counselors liked having dogs at the center. Her counselor said that the canines seemed to have a calming effect on most of the veterans.

At first at the vet's center, Mom just saw an individual counselor. Mom said the counselor promised that she'd get mom into a therapy group with other veterans when there was an opening. When Mom finally got into a therapy group, it was late June. I was out of school, so there were times when she had to take me because she wouldn't let me stay home alone. I said I didn't mind. I could always listen to the radio in the van—something I loved to do. That worked for a while, but one day it was so nice that I just couldn't stay put. The vet center was on a beautiful spot with a big garden and nearby pond. I hoped Mom wouldn't mind if I just went over and sat by the pond. Sometimes she seemed overly protective since she got home and wanted to know where I was every minute. I always tried to let her know. But the pond wasn't far from the van, and it wouldn't be easy to let her know I was going there, so I figured it would be okay

Sitting under a big tree next to the pond, I could watch the ducks and sometimes a little fish silvery in sunlight, splashing back into the water making little ripples. A big old frog sat on the bank croaking away, but when I moved, he hopped into the water and sped off. As I watched, a mother duck swam toward me with her babies following her. Several other ducks joined her. It was neat to watch them glide across the pond.

"Hey there, young lady, I thought you were staying in the van," my mom's voice startled me. With Spark sniffing and finding inviting places to lift his leg as they approached us, she rolled her wheelchair down the path that circled the pond. She had clipped on his thirty-foot leash that allowed him to go a little distance from her while still in her control. He had been trained at ABL that the longer leash and a command from Mom let him go further from her. Spark had also learned to untangle himself if he wound himself around a tree or bush. Mom almost never had to wheel up to him and get him untangled.

I looked out over the pond. It was across the drive from the vet center up a paved path that circled around the pond. The bushes and two large trees on the grassy knoll above the pond seemed great for just hanging out.

I was sorry that I did not have some bread to feed the ducks I saw swimming at the far end of the pond. I glanced at Mom, who was also watching the ducks. Had she forgotten that I was supposed to stay in the van?

"But, it's so warm and nice," I protested, just in case she was going to chew me out. Mom smiled and sighed. I think she thought it was nice, too.

"I guess it's okay. Just stay here and don't go too near the water. I know I can trust you. We had a break in our session, and Spark wanted to go

out, so we came to see what you were up to. I was concerned when I didn't see you in the van."

Just then Spark stopped, perked up his ears, and looked a little way down the pond. Unlike the well-behaved dog he was, Spark dashed past me and down the path to another tree nearby. He stopped, intent on something leaning against the tree. It was then that we heard crying. One thing we had learned about Spark is that he is very sensitive to

people's emotions. If I cry at home, he will come to me as if he wants to help. We looked where Spark stood beside someone, and there against another tree huddled a boy about my age. He buried his head in his knees drawn up to his chest. He seemed to be crying. I hadn't seen him before.

"Are you okay?" my mom called out. Wiping his face quickly with his sleeve, the boy looked up.

"I'm fine!" he croaked almost angrily and turned away.

"Maybe he needs to be alone," Mom told me with concern in her voice. She looked as if she really wanted to go to the boy, but it would also have been tough to wheel her chair off the path and into the grass near the pond where he was.

"This is a place that brings out a lot of emotions in people." She glanced at her watch. Evidently she was late for something or maybe she wasn't sure how to help the boy.

"Goodness! We had better get back. My break from group is over. Let's go, Spark," and her dog came dashing back in our direction. She hooked on Spark's normal leash and tugged the exercise leash into the pack she carried on her wheelchair.

"Now stay here, and I will be back soon," she told me as she blew me a kiss.

"Spark, heel!" she commanded, and they were gone, headed back into the vet center. I glanced quickly back at the boy. He sat pitching pebbles into the pond. He seemed angry.

"Hey! Don't hit the ducks!" I called to him.

"They're just stupid old ducks!" he yelled back. I got up and went toward him.

"What's your problem?" I asked. "They have more right to be here than we do!" Mom always said I was ready to stand up for something I believed in. It was probably silly to approach an angry boy as I did, but sometimes I act first and think later. But as I started toward him, he slumped again just like a balloon when all the air has gone out. As I got closer, I could see he was crying again. He wiped his face as if he didn't want me to see.

"Your mom or dad going here?" I asked quietly. His dark face streaked with tears despite his efforts to wipe them away. He was about as big as me with curly black hair and deep brown eyes. Kind of cute, even.

"Hi, I'm Sunny—short for Sunshine. I think my grandmother was some kind of hippy and suggested the name to Mom. Gram died a couple of years ago, but . . . " Why did I babble on to this kid? Maybe he looked like he needed a friend.

"My dad," he mumbled almost under his breath.

"Your dad? Your dad what?"

"You asked me who was coming to the vet center," he snapped.

"Okay! Okay! Don't take my head off. If you'd rather be alone, I get the hint," and I started to turn away.

"No! Wait! I'm sorry. I'm Malcolm, and my dad comes here. I don't mean to be a jerk. It's just that there's a lot of stuff going on."

I sat down beside Malcolm and watched the ducks. They were far enough away that he couldn't have hit them, and I thought they were keeping their distance.

"It's okay," I said. "I get 'stuff.' We have stuff, too. How can you not when your parent was a soldier and got hurt?"

"Your dad got hurt, too?" He looked at me intently.

"My mom. And yes, she injured her spine." It was the first time I had really told anyone. As I did, I felt a little twinge. What was it? Sadness? I didn't know. We had adjusted so well, partly because Mom tried so hard to be cheerful that none of the rest of us felt we could be sad. My Uncle Bob, who had been in the Army too, once told me that it was a "soldier thing" to try to act strong around other people.

"Wow!" said Malcolm. "How is that?" What a dumb question, I thought. But I just said, "It's been rough, but we're making it." Then a thought came to me, and I brightened.

"We have a service dog named Spark! Well, he's my mom's dog, really, to help her. She calls him her 'beloved tool.' She learned that from the agency where she got him—that he's a tool, like her wheelchair, but one she loves too. Spark's made a big difference."

But Malcolm was back in his own thoughts.

"I wish we were making it! Yesterday my mom said she is going to leave. She and Dad have been fighting something terrible since he got home. She said she couldn't take it anymore."

The ducks got braver, and I watched as the mother duck herded her babies nearer to her. I had all but lost my dad, and I knew that having a parent move away was tough.

"I'm sorry," I told Malcolm.

"Yeah, thanks. It's just that I get on with my dad better than I do with my mom. She's always on my

case. Dad's more laid back. If she moves out, she'll go live with my grandparents, and I don't want that, either. Mom works all the time anyway. I think she'd rather be at work than home with me and my sisters." He took a breath. It had all come out in what seemed like one rush, and he literally hadn't had a chance to breathe.

"You have sisters?" Probably a dumb thing for me to say, but I didn't know how to help him with the other stuff.

"Yeah, two, Sherry and Joy. They're younger than me. They can be a pain sometimes, but I guess they're okay. What about you?"

"Nope, just me," I told him. "I always wanted to have brothers or sisters."

"You'd think differently if they were always getting into your stuff!" he said.

The ducks got downright brave. They swam right near us—maybe hoping that we had some food. Malcolm surprised me and pulled a package of crackers out of his pocket.

"These are squashed anyway," he said and handed me some crumbs to throw to the ducks. The mother duck let out a loud quack and dove at the crumbs while a bunch of other ducks suddenly appeared and competed for the prize. We threw more until the package was gone.

"Compliments of the vending machine inside," Malcolm laughed. I think he felt better. But then he said:

"Someone once told me that ducks look really peaceful on the surface of the water, but underneath their legs go a mile a minute just to keep them afloat. That's how I feel sometimes."

As I thought about it, I understood what he meant.

"Malcolm?" a deep male voice called. "Where are you?"

"There's my dad. I gotta go. Maybe I'll see you again?"

"Yes, that'd be good," I told him. I waved as he ran off toward a big man who looked a lot like Malcolm except that he walked on metal crutches. Even at a distance, I could see him wince with pain. No sooner had Malcolm and his dad driven off than Mom and Spark came out of the building.

"Find a friend?" she asked, obviously having seen Malcolm and me together.

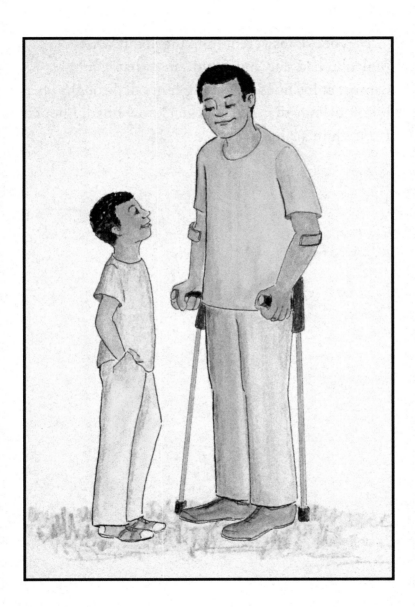

"Maybe," I answered, thinking about what Malcolm had said and wondering what would happen at his house. Hearing him talk brought up a lot of feelings that I didn't even know I had. I hoped I'd see him again.

I Have an Idea

The next time Mom had her veterans group, I was at my friend Dora's, so I didn't go. The next week I had a really bad cold, and Mom thought I should stay home. Aunt June came over while Mom was gone, so I didn't go with Mom and Spark to the vet center for a couple of weeks. As we drove up to the building, I wondered if Malcolm was there and glanced over at the pond. I was disappointed not to see him.

Mom maneuvered her chair onto the ramp, rolled out of the van, and got Spark out and ready to work.

"You can walk over to the pond, but the same

thing applies as last time. Don't wander off, get into anyone's car, or go too near the pond. Understand?"

I nodded. The safety speech was familiar.

"Maybe you'll see your friend," Mom called back as she wheeled toward the building.

"Don't see him," I called after her, and at that very moment I did. He came out from behind a tree near the pond and tossed a last pebble into the water as he came toward me.

"Don't hit the . . . " I started.

"Ducks!" he finished. "I won't. The babies are a lot bigger. Come see." He urged me toward the pond. Sure enough, there were the ducks, and the ducklings had certainly grown. Their fuzzy little bodies had some feathers. We plunked down by the water's edge and watched the mother duck, her babies, and a couple of other ducks glide calmly across the water.

"Today I got some bread," said Malcolm reaching in his pocket and bringing out a somewhat squashed Baggie. He handed me a slice, and together we threw bits into the water and enjoyed the antics of the ducks as they fought for the pieces of bread as

they turned soggy and started to sink. The momma duck always managed to swim between her babies and the bigger ducks so that the little ones had an opportunity to grab some of the bread bits.

"Look at that! She's really taking care of them!" I exclaimed. Malcolm said nothing, and I looked over at him. His face did not look as cheerful as it had when he greeted me. Suddenly realizing he must be thinking of his mom, I felt bad.

"So what's new?" I asked feebly, although we both knew I was having difficulty covering up a tense moment.

"She's moving out at the end of August," he said softly. "My sisters are going with her."

"Your mom's leaving?" Then I realized how unnecessary that had been. Of course his mom.

Malcolm said nothing. He just stared at the ducks.

"Malcolm, I'm sorry." I hoped when I grew up I'd be better able to handle such moments. I felt like anything I said would be the wrong thing. But Malcolm smiled weakly.

"Yeah. It's a bummer."

Suddenly a thought came to me. Oh, no! Did that mean that Malcolm was going away too? I realized how much I had been looking forward to seeing him. I'd just met him, and now I might be losing him. That wouldn't feel good at all. Finally I found the words for the question that was so hard to ask.

"And what about you?"

Malcolm said nothing as he threw his last piece of bread into the water. A big duck pushed the others out of the way and dove for it. The losers squawked loudly as they looked up at us as if to beg for more.

"Sorry, guys," said Malcolm. "That's it 'til next time."

We sat quietly for a bit until the ducks lost interest in us and began to swim away. Malcolm sighed deeply.

"Don't know," he began. "I told my dad I want to stay with him, but Mom thinks I should go with her. We live in an apartment, and she complains that it is too small. I think that's part of it. She hates where we live, and that makes things even worse between Mom and Dad." He watched the ducks as they swam away from us as if they knew Malcolm didn't have any more bread.

"Mom and my sisters will live with my grand-parents. They're okay, but I'd rather stay with my dad. Mom says he can't possibly take care of me . . . because of the way he is now." He barely whispered the last few words.

"'Cause he got hurt?" I asked. "Mom takes care of me just fine. And I help her out, too. Why couldn't you do that for your dad?"

"It's not just his leg," Malcolm began. "He got blown up in this blast in Iraq. It wrecked his leg but it also did something to his head. They call it traumatic brain injury or TBI. He can't think as fast as he used to. And he gets frustrated when he can't and really angry sometimes. That's why he comes here." He gestured to the vet center building.

I thought of how frustrated my mom got sometimes. She'd been an athlete before she got hurt. She used to run every morning, and we'd go mountain climbing sometimes, too. I thought about how angry she sometimes got when she couldn't do something she used to be able to do. It made her snap at me sometimes. Aunt June said that we really had to give her space when she needed it. Having her life changed wasn't easy for Mom to take.

"Sometimes we just have to be patient," I heard myself saying. Now where did that come from?

"My mom has tough times, too," I said. I found myself telling my friend, Malcolm, about what it was like when my mom first came home. She cried a lot in her room even though she tried to be cheerful around me. She had to learn how to do everyday things all over again. She went to physical therapy to re-learn how to dress herself and cook and clean. We had someone come in to clean, but in the beginning Mom tried to do it all. Sometimes she'd get frustrated and yell at me. Then she'd apologize and tell me how hard it was to learn a new way of life.

Mom found a therapist at a local mental health center and she told me that the therapist was really helping her adjust to her disability and to understand some of her reactions to things she'd seen in the military. But then her therapist got a job somewhere else. Since there was no one else at the clinic who knew much about working with veterans the clinic referred Mom to the veteran's center. Mom liked coming to the vet center. She told me that being in a group with other veterans and having a new therapist who was trained to work with veterans really helped her.

And then there was Spark. He had made so much difference in our lives. Not only did he help her with tasks like retrieving things and opening doors and turning on light switches, but he woke her from nightmares and cheered her up. She'd seemed much better since she had gotten Spark. Then it hit me.

"Hey, your dad needs to get a service dog like Spark! That could really help him!"

"A dog! Cool. I'd play catch with him and . . . " Malcolm brightened.

"No, no, no! Not that kind of dog, silly. Not a pet for you. A helper dog for your dad. Spark goes everywhere with Mom and helps her with stuff. Sometimes he knows what she's going to do before she even does it."

It was true. Sometimes Spark would bring Mom his leash when the next thing she intended to do was take him out or bring her the keys when she was just about to go to the store.

"I don't know," said Malcolm, obviously less enthusiastic.

"Just think about it!" I told him. "You can talk to my mom, and then you'll be convinced that it's a great idea!"

As if on cue, my mom came out of the vet center with Spark.

"Hi, guys," she greeted us. "Having fun?" As she approached I could see that Malcolm was dying to pet Spark.

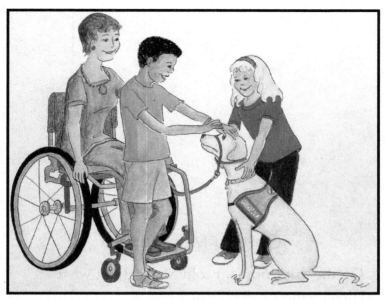

"Can I pet him?" he finally got the courage to ask.

"Sure," said Mom and then to Spark, "Go say hello." Wagging his long tail, Spark greeted Malcolm, who ruffled his fur and laughed.

"He's great!" cried Malcolm and I knew that our plan to get his dad a service dog was a good one.

Getting Mom's Help

On the drive home, I told Mom about what Malcolm and I had talked about.

"Getting a service dog is a big step, Sunny. It's not for everyone. Maybe Malcolm's father—" She interrupted herself and said, "Gabe is his name, by the way. He's in my group. Maybe he wouldn't be interested," my mom said.

"Couldn't you just talk to him? Tell him how great Spark has been for you?" I begged.

"Maybe, but . . . " Then Mom got that look that she has when she gets an idea.

"A lot of the veterans in my group have asked about Spark. Maybe the folks from ABL would come and talk about service dogs." I knew that ABL was Assistance Dogs for Better Living, the agency that had trained Spark and placed him with my mom.

"Great!! How soon can you call them?" I exclaimed.

"Goodness! Hold your horses!"

"But I know a dog could help him," I protested.

"We'll see," Mom said. "I'll call when we get home."

Mom was as good as her word. She was on the phone to ABL as soon as we got home. When she finished her call, I was right there.

"So? What did they say?" I think I was bouncing up and down, because she laughed and told me to sit down. I tend to get really excited when something interests me.

"They'll call the vet center and see if they are interested in having a speaker on service dogs, and then we'll see what happens." Mom told me.

"Thanks, Mom!" I hugged her and almost knocked her out of her chair.

"Careful! And don't get your hopes up."

I was anxious to see Malcolm again and to tell him what Mom had suggested.

"Hey, guess what?" I greeted him the next week. I told him all about Mom calling ABL.

"That's great. But I don't know if my dad will want to get a dog," Malcolm said skeptically.

"Doesn't he like dogs?" I could not believe that anyone would not like a dog.

"He loves dogs," said Malcolm as he watched an ant crawl up his pant leg.

"Look at that," he commented, pointing at the ant. "I must seem like a mountain to him." We were sitting by the pond again and watching the sky. I hoped it wouldn't rain before our parents got out of their group.

"Well, just talk to him about Spark and how great he is," I told him. Malcolm had petted Spark a few times since that first time when my mom came out before his dad. Spark really seemed to like my friend, too.

"It's just that Dad said this morning that there have been too many changes, and we just have to get used to things again. He said I could stay with him when my mom moves out. Mom isn't happy, but she finally agreed. She's moving in a few weeks. She wants to get my sisters signed up for school so they'll be ready when it starts. I'll miss them, but I'd rather stay with Dad. We just get on better. Mom's always on my case."

Malcolm seemed relieved but sad at the same time. It must be hard to know your mom is leaving. At least my dad left before I was really old enough to think about it.

"Maybe it would be a help having a dog. That's a good kind of change," I said, but Malcolm had gone back to studying the ant and giving it things to climb over like his finger and a leaf, as it crawled up his leg.

The next two weeks that Mom went to group, it rained, and we couldn't stay out by the pond. But Mom spoke with the receptionist who said Malcolm and I could stay in the waiting room and watch TV. There wasn't much on, so we played a video game Malcolm had brought with him. Getting bored with the game, I looked around the waiting room and read a few of the notices posted on a big

Talk By —
ASSISTANCE DOGS
for
BETTER LIVING

July 22

board. "Hey, look at this!!" I grabbed Malcolm's
sleeve and almost made him drop video game.
Annoyed, he grabbed it.

"Come 'ere!" I said.

"Wait! I'm almost at another level," he said glancing at the game back in his hands. "Oh, darn! You made me lose." He put the game back in his pocket and came over to me.

"Look at this poster," I said. "It says 'Talk by Assistance Dogs for Better Living, July 22.' Hey that's next week!" I told him.

"Your mom did it," said Malcolm. "That's great. And look at this. 'Families Invited.' Hey, awesome! We can come, too!"

We were so excited by the poster that we hardy heard Mom and Malcolm's dad come up behind us. I felt a cold nose on my bare leg and realized that Spark was there, too.

"What has you kids so excited?" asked Mom.

"Can we go to the talk?" Malcolm and I chimed at once.

Mom smiled. "What do you think, Gabe?" she asked Malcolm's father, who was right behind her hobbling painfully on his metal crutches.

"Shall we let these kids go?" Gabe smiled too.

"I don't see why not," he said cheerfully. Malcolm and I looked at each other. I winked.

We Learn about Service Dogs

Malcolm and I couldn't wait for the demon-stration to begin as we sat in the meeting room of the vet's center a week later. Mom and Malcolm's dad sat together further back, but we'd gotten a front row seat. Marge, one of the staff we had met at Assistance Dogs for Better Living when Mom got Spark, brought some posters and fliers about service dogs.

"I want to thank you for this chance to talk with you," she said. "We're going to be informal today, so please feel free to ask questions. Let me tell you a little bit about our agency. Assistance Dogs for

Better Living, or A-B-L—pronounced 'able'—trains and places service dogs with people experiencing all types of disabilities."

"My uncle has a dog to help him. He's blind," piped up a boy in the second row.

"Ah, yes," said Marge. "That is called a guide dog and is different from a service dog."

"How?" someone else asked.

"It is in their temperaments—their personalities. Guide dogs have to take charge in some situations. For example, if the person told his guide dog to cross a street not knowing that a car was coming, the guide dog knows to stop and let his person know not to cross right then. We use more assertive dogs for guide dog work," Marge explained.

"Like German Shepherds? That's what my uncle has," said the boy in the second row.

"That's right. But service dogs are different in temperament. We use Labrador Retrievers or Golden Retrievers mostly for service dog work. They are more laid back and depend upon getting a command. If you took a service dog into a busy street and told him to cross it, he'd respond to the command—car or no car."

"Squish!" said the boy. Then he seemed to think twice about his comment and looked around.

"Sorry," he whispered.

"It would not be good," Marge continued. "But then people who have service dogs are not blind, so it would not be an issue. Service dogs help with other things. Let's see a service dog in action." Marge looked toward the back of the room and gestured. To my surprise my mom and Spark approached Marge.

"I usually bring a dog to demonstrate some of what service dogs can do," Marge was saying, "but I knew that you have someone here who can show us. I have asked Amanda Carter, one of your own veterans, to demonstrate with her service dog, Spark."

Wow! I thought this could not have been better. Mom turned her chair around to face the audience, and Spark, all dressed in his ABL vest and looking up at Mom expectantly, sat by her side.

"Now as you can see, there are some things that could be tough for Amanda to reach while she is in her chair. So—what if she dropped her keys?"

Mom pulled her keys from her pocket and casually dropped them in front of her chair far enough away that she would not be able to reach them. Spark snapped to attention, looking at the keys and then at my mom.

"Fetch them!" Mom commanded. Instantly Spark grabbed the keys. It challenged him to get the metal, but Mom had a soft ball on her key ring that made it easy for him to grab.

"Hold!" said Mom, and Spark brought the keys to her. "Give!" Spark easily let Mom take the keys from his mouth. Murmurs of appreciation filled the room.

"You will notice," Marge began, "that Spark is wearing a vest that says ABL—the agency that trained him—and 'assistance dog.' That is to let people know that he is a service dog and his owner has valid reason to bring him into places that would otherwise not allow dogs. These dogs are trained to understand that when they are wearing their vests that they are on duty."

"Do they have to wear the vest all the time?" asked someone.

"Only when they are out in public," Marge explained. "It is like a uniform. At home they don't have to wear the vest. And at play, they don't wear a vest. Their owners do not expect them to perform service functions when they are at play."

"What else can a service dog do?" someone else asked. Marge looked at Mom.

"Why don't you tell them, Amanda?" Mom looked a bit flustered. I am not sure that she knew she was going to talk.

"Well," Mom began, "I am forever leaving my cell phone places and forgetting where I put it. Spark is great at finding it and giving it to me."

Mom handed Marge her phone so that Spark didn't see her. As Mom continued talking, Marge moved casually to the back of the room and put the phone down on the floor under a chair.

"And if I want a water or a soda from fridge, I can tell Spark to get it," Mom explained.

Marge had brought a little portable refrigerator. A thick cord attached to the handle. Mom wheeled her chair nearer to the fridge with Spark at her side.

"Tug!" she told Spark, who grabbed the cord and pulled open the fridge door.

"Fetch it!" Mom said, and the dog grabbed a bottle of water and took it to Mom. Then on another command, Spark went back and closed the door of the fridge.

The room erupted in applause. Spark sat by Mom's side and looked out at the crowd as if to say, "What happened? What did I miss?" That got a laugh from everyone.

Mom's phone rang somewhere in the back of the room. I noticed Marge's own phone in her hand: she must have called Mom's number.

"Get it!" Mom told Spark. Eagerly he set off, sniffing the floor, the chairs, and even the people until he discovered the phone beneath a chair. With a wag of his tail, he picked it up and raced back to Mom. You could almost see how excited he was that he found it.

"Good boy!" Mom praised, ruffling his fur, taking the phone, and giving him a treat.

Marge talked about other things that service dogs could do, and Spark demonstrated some of them.

"But perhaps one of the most important things that a service dog can do for someone with a disability is this," explained Marge as she helped Mom slide out of her wheelchair and onto the floor.

"Let's say you have fallen out of your chair. What do you do?" asked Marge.

"Spark can summon help," Mom said as she lay on the floor.

"Spark, speak!" Spark let out several sharp barks meant to alert someone.

"So let's say there is no one nearby," said Marge. "Is there any other way he could help?."

Mom sat up, called Spark to her, and positioned her wheelchair behind her.

"Spark, brace!" she told the dog. Spark positioned himself and stood still and rigid so that Mom could pull herself up into her chair using Spark for balance. When she had sat back in her chair, everyone applauded. She gave Spark another treat and praised him.

"That has really been a help," Mom explained, tearing up. "I used to wonder what I would ever do if I fell out of my chair and no one was around. With Spark, I don't have to worry. He's become one of my best friends." She buried her head in her dog's fur, and I wanted to cry, too. I looked over at Malcolm. His eyes also looked moist, but I pretended not to notice.

After Marge's talk, people had all kinds of questions. Malcolm's dad looked really interested.

"How does someone get one of these dogs?" a veteran asked.

Marge gave him her phone number and the ABL website, and we saw Malcolm's dad hurriedly jot it down. Malcolm and I looked at each other. Malcolm had the biggest smile.

Moving Ahead

Soon after the talk by ABL Malcolm told me excitedly that his dad had gotten an application for a service dog and had submitted it.

"My mom wasn't happy," Malcolm told me. "She said that all he needed was one more thing to take care of. Dad told her all about what he learned at the meeting and showed her the pamphlets they got from ABL, and she seemed to calm down."

Malcolm was quiet for a minute and then continued. "When Dad was out of the room, Mom told me that I had to help him out, because she wouldn't be there. It made me really sad. I don't

want her and my sisters to leave. I hear my mom and dad arguing a lot about it now. Dad keeps trying to find ways to get her to stay. I think he hoped that she would see that he was getting help and want to stick it out, but . . ." He didn't finish and just looked off in the distance.

It was a rainy day, and Mom said that Malcolm and I could sit in the van and listen to the radio while she and Malcolm's dad were at their group. The dreary day seemed to add to Malcolm's sad mood. I felt bad for him. I would hate to have my mom move away.

It was nearing the end of August when Malcolm met me outside the vet center one day and seemed excited.

"What's up?" I asked.

"Dad heard from that dog place," he told me. He seemed excited and happy about it.

"ABL?"

"Yeah, ABL. They want him to come in for an interview. They said that he was a good candidate for a dog!"

"Great!" I told him. I felt almost as excited as he was that our plan was moving ahead.

"And," Malcolm went on, "we're moving."

"Where?" I asked, worried that his dad might want to go to a different vet center and we wouldn't see each other.

"We're renting a house," Malcolm continued. He was obviously excited and maybe didn't realize that we might not be able to see each other if the new place was too far away.

"Dad says it will be great. And he's convinced Mom to stay and move into the house with us. I think she's going to do it. She says that even applying for this dog has put Dad in a better mood so he isn't just moping around like he was. That drove Mom nuts."

Malcolm was almost laughing as he told me his news.

"That's great," I said. I was happy for Malcolm, but I was still concerned.

"Where?" I asked again.

"Where? Oh . . . " I think it dawned on him what the move might mean.

"I know that it is a way from where we live now. I have to change schools. But that's okay. I wasn't crazy about the one I was going to. The kids were really mean. I hated it."

"I'm sorry," I said. One kid in my neighborhood had said something about my mom once, and I stood up to him till he backed down. Uncle Bob was over to cut our lawn, and he told the kid to leave. He told me that Mom had served her country and I should be very proud.

"Yeah, he was right, I guess," he said.

"So where is the house?" I asked again.

"It's near a park where Dad says we can play, and there's a dog park where we can exercise Dad's dog." He smiled shyly. "When we get it."

"The place is called Silver Park," he went on. "I remembered that because the street the house is on is called Silver, too, and. . . . "

"Silver Park?! Silver Street? That's right near my house!" I was jumping up and down with excitement

"Really?" Malcolm looked surprised. "You're kidding, right?"

"No! We're two streets over on Chapman Street! And you'd go to my school!"

"No way!"

"Way!" I squealed in excitement.

"What are you kids so excited about?" I hadn't even heard Mom and Malcolm's dad come up behind us as we sat by the pond—or we *had* been sitting until Malcolm gave me his news and I was so excited that I jumped up and danced up and down. Malcolm had sprung to his feet, too, and was just as excited as I was.

"They're moving near us!" I exclaimed.

"Yes, I know," said Mom. "Gabe was telling us in group, and I realized where they were moving is right near us. That's great. I told Gabe that maybe we can help them move. Aunt June and Uncle Bob might be glad to help, too."

"We do appreciate that, Amanda," Malcolm's dad said. "I think these two young folks will really have fun when we move. And maybe Gloria and I can have you over once we're settled."

As he said it I remembered the other part of Malcolm's news, that his mom, Gloria, had agreed to give them another chance to be together. I was so glad. Things really seemed to be looking up.

Next Steps

At the end of August, Mom, Uncle Bob, Aunt June, and I helped Malcolm and his family move into their new house.

Malcolm had a big room to himself. He couldn't wait to show it to me along with the rest of the house. He could put up all of his sports posters in this place.

There was a small, grassy, fenced-in back yard, and Malcolm showed me where he thought the dog could run when they got it. A lot of his conversation now started "When Dad gets his dog . . . " I hoped that all went well.

"Mom's worried about having a yard," Malcolm said. "She says that Dad can't mow it and she can't 'cause she has a grass allergy." Malcolm told me.

"That's not a problem," I said. "Mom can't do ours. Uncle Bob used to mow it for us, but he showed me how, and sometimes I do it. These lawns are so small that it's not that hard."

"Will you show me how?" he asked quietly. "Sure," I told him. I felt good that I could help him.

A few weeks later, school started again after the summer vacation. It was also the day Malcolm's dad was supposed to hear back from ABL. He had gone a week before for an interview, and they said they would let him know by that day if he was accepted to get a dog.

It was great introducing Malcolm to the kids at school. Everyone I knew was friendly to him, and I thought he'd fit in well. My buddy Austin found out that Malcolm liked to shoot baskets, so he asked him to meet him at Silver Park sometime and shoot a few. I could tell that Malcolm really liked my friends, and that made me feel good.

"Call me when you find out if your dad is getting a dog," I told Malcolm as we walked from school to his house and I continued on toward my own street

"I will," he called back.

At home, Mom greeted me and quizzed me about my first day of school. I told her all about introducing Malcolm to everyone and how I thought he'd fit in.

"You're a good friend, my Sunny," she said. "I'm proud of you."

"Aw, Mom," I said, and inside I felt really good.

I looked over my homework for a while. Homework on the first day of school! Ugh. But it was math, and I was pretty good in math, so it was easy. Still, it was hard to concentrate. I kept waiting for the phone to ring and for Malcolm to tell me the news.

Spark nosed at my leg as if to say "Don't worry." He picked up on my feelings as well as my mom's. When he was home and not wearing his service dog vest, he usually stayed near Mom anyway, but sometimes he'd check out what I was up to.

But if Mom called or he sensed that she needed something, he was right there at her side.

"You're a good ole mutt," I told him as I stroked his ears. They were so soft.

Just then the phone rang, and I think we both jumped. Spark was alert, looking at Mom to see if he was supposed to get the phone, but I beat him to it.

"I'll get it!" I sang out almost tripping over Spark in my haste to get the phone—wherever it was. I could hear it ring, but where the heck had we put it? Did Spark really smile, or was it my imagination as he gleefully ran to the couch and fished the phone out from between the cushions? Of course, he took it to Mom just as he'd been trained to do.

"Hello?" Mom handed Spark a treat and glanced at me. I thought the dog looked smug.

"Yes, Malcolm. She's right here," Mom chuckled as she handed me the phone. "Waiting for this call?" she teased.

I hardly got the phone to my ear when I heard Malcolm's excited voice ringing out, "He's accepted! Dad's getting a dog!!!"

"Yes!!!" I said, and Mom and I high-fived.

Waiting

We all had a hard time waiting after that phone call. With Malcolm's dad (who told me I should call him Gabe instead of Mr. Davis) accepted by ABL, we waited to hear about a date for his training. Gabe had to go to the ABL campus for two weeks where he would meet his dog and learn how to work with him.

I remember when Mom went for her training and to get Spark. It felt like the longest two weeks of my life. I hated waiting.

In the next few weeks, we kids got into school activities. Malcolm and I were in the same class, and sometimes we did homework together. Sometimes I went to his house after school, and sometimes he came over to mine. Our friends Madison and Taylor and Austin met at the park on Saturdays, and we shot baskets. I loved sports and hoped that I could swim and be a runner some day like Mom was before she got hurt.

The Davises started going to a church near us, and Malcolm invited me. We used to go to church but hadn't for a while. I'm not sure why. I liked the Sunday School and talked Mom into coming with me.

Our families had become friends, and that was great. I think that Mom and Gabe helped each other and maybe it was also good for Malcolm's mom, Gloria, to see how independent my mom was.

It turned out that Gloria and Mom had a lot in common, and they became good friends. Sometimes they went shopping together, and Gloria taught Mom how to make jewelry. Some evenings Gloria came over with all kinds old beads and supplies and gave Mom a lesson. Pretty soon, Mom got hooked, and she bought some really pretty beads, wire, and tools. She and Gloria made necklaces and bracelets

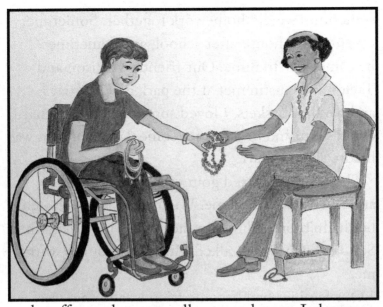

and stuff together—usually at our house. I always hoped that Malcolm would come, but Gloria said he was a big help getting his little sisters Sherry and Joy to bed. I wondered if she thought Gabe couldn't do it.

Malcolm said that his mom wasn't always sure how to act around his dad despite the time that had passed since his dad came home. Sometimes, she tried to help too much, and Gabe got mad. Other times, she'd get busy doing other things and seemed almost to ignore him.

Gloria worked a lot, too, in a lawyer's office as a receptionist or assistant or something. Sometimes she worked late, and Malcolm and the girls helped get supper.

Malcolm said his parents seemed happier, but he still heard them argue sometimes when they thought everyone was asleep. Gloria still wasn't sure the dog was a good idea, and I think they fought about that, too.

"Mom says the dog will end up being one more thing for her to take care of. But Dad says the dog will be his to care for. I don't think Mom is convinced. Then she complains that there'll be dog hair all over the house. Dad just shakes his head and says, 'We'll deal with it.'" Malcolm paused and looked like he was fighting back tears.

"I just hope that Mom doesn't decide to move out after all," he said quietly.

September became October, and Malcolm, the other kids, and I tried to figure out what to be for Halloween. Mom said that we were going to be too old to go trick or treating in a couple of years so we'd better make these costumes good ones. In the end Malcolm decided to be a ninja, and I planned to be a clown. I had seen some at a circus once, and I loved their silly costumes.

"That shouldn't be much of a stretch," Mom laughed. "You're already a clown!"

"Thanks, Mom!"

Mom and Aunt June had a great time sewing together a costume, and Malcolm and I got some makeup at Walmart to paint our faces. Gloria came over to help us figure out how to get made up. She was better at it than my mom.

"What's a ninja look like?" I asked Malcolm. He took out the video game he was always playing. I never took too much notice of it because it always seemed to distract him from the stuff we were doing.

"Like this," he showed me.

"Ugh!" I responded

He just laughed.

At home that night, Mom helped figure out what part of my costume I could wear at school for our party the next day. They wouldn't let me wear face paint, so we also figured out how I would add face makeup that night when we went trick or treating.

The phone rang.

"I'll get it!" I called out. As usual, Spark looked at Mom to see if he should get it.

"Okay," she said to me, and then, to Spark, "Leave it, Boy."

It was Malcolm. When he was excited, he had a way of blurting things out the moment I picked up the phone before I even had a chance to say hello.

"Dad got the training dates!"

I knew immediately what he meant but said, "To go to ABL for his dog?"

"Yes! And they sent him a picture. Her name is Lexi, and she's a Golden Retriever. She's really pretty!" Malcolm sounded excited.

"So when does he go?"

"The first week of December! What a Christmas present." Someone said something in the background, and Malcolm paused.

"Oh, right," he said to the voice, obviously his dad. "My dad wants to talk to your mom."

After Gabe told Mom and asked her a bunch of questions about the training, they let us talk again. Malcolm chattered on about how excited he was.

"Don't forget that it's your dad's dog," I couldn't help but remind him. It was something I had to learn when Spark first came home, that he was first of all Mom's helper dog. Once we settled in, he liked me, too, but Mom always counted as his number one. That's how he was trained.

"Yeah, I know," Malcolm admitted, sounding subdued. "But I see how much he does for your mom . . ." He trailed off, and I knew that he hoped that having a service dog would make things better at his house, too.

We had a great time that Halloween. After we kids trick or treated, the Davises invited Mom and me back to their house. Everyone seemed to be in a really good mood, and Gabe even joked that his costume was "a future service dog owner," even though he wasn't wearing anything special.

November was more exciting than ever as we all thought about Gabe's new dog. That Thanksgiving, we invited the Davises to our house and Aunt June and Uncle Bob, too. Gabe and Gloria had gotten to know my aunt and uncle at family get-togethers, and Uncle Bob sometimes went over and helped Gabe with things he couldn't do around the house.

We had a great day. Mom, Gloria and Aunt June cooked a great meal of turkey, stuffing, and mashed potatoes—vegetables, too. They had Gabe carve up the turkey even though he said he wasn't very good at it. He wasn't, but it tasted good anyway. I helped Mom make a pumpkin pie, and Aunt June brought an apple one. Dinner was great, and we laughed about Sherry's version of the first Thanksgiving that she learned in school. She had it confused with the story about Christopher Columbus discovering America, but everyone told her she was a great story teller, and she looked happy. Joy was quieter or too busy eating. That kid could sure eat!

"Come on. Let's get these dishes cleaned up," said Uncle Bob in his usual encouraging way. "Come on, Sunny and Malcolm. You can help Gabe and me."

"You mean load the dishwasher?" Mom joked. "That's really tough!"

"Ah, but there is a knack to getting them all in," laughed Uncle Bob as Malcolm and I cleared the table and handed the dishes to Gabe, propped on one crutch. He then handed them off to Uncle Bob, who arranged them carefully in the dish washer.

"I can't wait to see the Pats play today," Said Gabe. "They're doing well this year."

"Better than last year," Uncle Bob responded as he fit the last plate into the dishwasher rack. We were New England Patriots fans—no one more so than Uncle Bob. Mom and I were big sports fans, too, and we had spent quite a few Sunday afternoons watching games with Uncle Bob while we ate popcorn on the couch. Aunt June said that football was kind of silly with everyone always getting into pig piles. That's what she called the tackles. She just went to do the crosswords or read while we watched.

That day, Malcolm, Gabe, Mom, Uncle Bob, and I watched the Patriots go on to victory over the Denver Broncos. Aunt June and Gloria, who wasn't a football fan either, busied themselves in the kitchen making snacks and talking. Sherry and Joy were sprawled out on the floor in the hall busily building something out of my old Legos set.

I went to the kitchen to get another drink and overheard Gloria.

"I hope Gabe can manage this training," she said. "He's in an awful lot of pain, though he'd never let on. I worry about him. Sometimes his TBI-his traumatic brain injury—means that he can't remember things. I try to remind him, and he snaps at me. How is he going to remember things when he gets this dog?"

"I'm sure he'll do fine, dear. He really seems to want this dog, and that will help," Aunt June responded in her soothing voice that helped me after we learned about Mom getting hurt. "The people at ABL understand disabilities and TBI. They know how to work with people who have lost the ability to do things they did comfortably before, and they can advise about how to compensate for limitations."

"Having a service dog will help Gabe—not necessarily with the pain, but if anything should happen . . . " she saw me and broke off.

"Hi there, Sunny. What do you need, dear?"

"Another juice, please. And one for Malcolm too."

"Apple or grape?"

"Grape, please." She smiled and handed me a couple of small bottles of juice out of the fridge. Spark wandered into the kitchen and wagged his tail, coming to me for a pat. He seemed to feel he was officially off duty while Mom and the others rooted for their team in loud and excited voices.

"I should have had this handsome fellow get the juice for you," Aunt June laughed. I wondered if she was reminding Gloria of all the things the dog could do.

"He's Mom's dog," I told her with a little smile. "He only does that for her." Spark gazed up at me. Was he saying, "I'd get it for you if you asked." Who knows?

After the football game on TV, Malcolm, Uncle Bob, Gloria, Aunt June, and I played Boggle, a word game that Mom got me because she said it would improve my spelling. I don't know about that, but we had fun playing it. Gabe and Mom sat talking together in their chairs by the couch. I could hear bits of the conversation and knew that Gabe was asking her about the training.

"What if I can't remember the commands for the dog?" I heard Gabe ask.

"The trainers at ABL understand TBI," Mom told him. "They told the veterans who have it to bring a notebook and jot things down. You'll train with a group of veterans, Gabe. Everyone is in a similar boat. TBI, PTSD—post-traumatic stress disorder, physical disabilities: we all have something. I was diagnosed with a mild case of PTSD when I first got home. Now that's pretty well under control. I'm not always nervous about anyone sneaking up on me. Spark has my back. Lexi will be there for you, too."

"I guess so," Gabe began. "I'm just worried that I won't be good for her."

Mom smiled. "A lot of us feel that way, Gabe. But just look at Spark." Hearing his name, Mom's dog sat up and looked at her expectantly waiting for further instruction.

"Spark, visit!" she said, and the dog came and looked up at her as he rested his head on her leg. She fondly stroked his ear

"He's good for me," Mom said, "and I'm good for him. We're a team, and you and Lexi will be too."

Our Boggle game got really exciting then, so I didn't hear any more. But I thought about what Mom had said as I lay in bed that night. I wondered what difference their service dog would make in the Davis' lives as Spark had in ours.

Lexi

Malcolm came over almost every day during the two weeks that Gabe was in training at ABL. He asked me a ton of questions. And then it was the day that Gabe and Lexi were to come home. I knew that Malcolm would be home that night but I was sure he'd call. When the phone rang about eight, I knew it was my friend.

"So how is it going?" I asked as he let me get in the first words.

"Great," he said not quite as excited as he had been. "Lexi is really pretty. But she looks at Dad all the time and Dad says that we can't play with her until she gets use to being here."

"Yeah, that's hard," I told him. "I remember that when Spark came home. He only went to Mom, and the rest of us didn't count!" we both laughed.

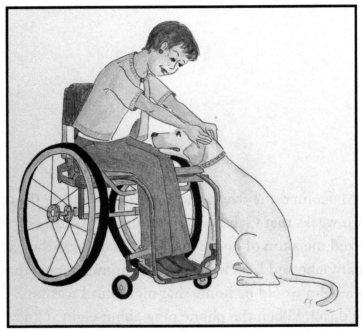

"Lexi's trained to respond only to your dad—her main person," I went on. "And he has to get use to depending on her. It gets better, I promise."

I knew Malcolm would be a little disappointed. No matter how much we told him this was his dad's helper, he was so excited about having a dog. But we'd had Spark for almost two years, and he was part of the family even though he was still Mom's helper.

"When can I see her?" I remembered that ABL had told us to make the first weekend we were home with Spark a low-key weekend without lots of people other than the family until he got used to us.

"Dad said he'd ask your mom and you to meet us at the dog park on Sunday afternoon. He wants to introduce Lexi to Spark."

I couldn't wait for Sunday. Finally, it came and Mom, Spark, and I met Malcolm, his dad and mom, and Lexi at the dog park at Silver Park. She was a beautiful dog with long, soft reddish hair. Spark perked up his ears, and Mom and Gabe let them meet slowly.

"What a gorgeous coat she has," Mom commented.

"And she sure does shed!" said Gloria. Then she looked at Gabe as if she had said something wrong, but he didn't seem to notice. He was too busy watching the dogs. The two dogs, used to being trained with other dogs, sniffed each other and

apparently decided they liked what they smelled, then made it clear that they wanted to play. We walked them around a bit just so they could get used to each other. They acted like old buddies.

"Well, that went well," Mom laughed as they let the dogs into the fenced-in dog park for a run. We were the only ones there, and we laughed a lot as Spark and Lexi chased and tackled each other.

"Well, Amanda, looks like the beginning of a beautiful friendship," Gabe commented with a chuckle. The dogs had a great run until it started to snow.

"Here comes the snow they've been promising," said Gabe.

"I think we should get home before it gets slippery." Gloria said nervously. Malcolm had told us that his dad sometimes had a hard time getting around with his metal crutches when the ground was slippery. Mom and Gabe called their dogs. They both came instantly as they had been trained.

"It always amazes me when Lexi obeys so quickly," Gabe said hooking her leash to her collar.

"That's how she was trained," Mom said as she put Spark's leash on him. "Lucky for us, huh?"

"Right!" Gabe responded as we started toward our homes. Malcolm and I tried to catch snowflakes on our tongues. He was better at it than me.

After Gabe got Lexi, Malcolm was not at my house as much. I realized that Spark had been one of the reasons why he liked to come over, but I knew that it was because he was my friend, too. Still, Malcolm called me most nights to tell me new things Lexi did. She did things that Spark did, too— like turn on or off the light switch and get stuff from the fridge. I knew it was all new to Malcolm, though, so I listened to everything he told me.

It wasn't long before Gabe let Malcolm play with Lexi, and he threw the ball or Frisbee for her to fetch. Of course, she always brought it back to Gabe as she was trained to do, but Malcolm

still liked to join in their play. When it wasn't
too slippery, Mom, Gabe, Malcolm, and I walked
the dogs together. Malcolm told me that on the
days when it was too treacherous to go out, Gabe
exercised Lexi on a treadmill that they had bought
just for that purpose.

"No way!" I said. "A dog on a treadmill!"

"Yes. ABL has started training their dogs to do
that," Mom interrupted when she heard us. "They
told me to bring in Spark sometime, and they'd try
him out on one. I should do that."

"We don't have a treadmill," I said. I thought that was an important piece to add to the conversation.

"I'm sure we could find a used one," Mom replied. I knew that for the last two winters Mom was often able to get out in her chair to walk Spark. But she wheeled the chair herself, and even with gloves, her hands got pretty cold. We'd had our small back yard fenced in so on the rare occasions that she couldn't get out, Spark still could.

Getting ready for Christmas that year was even more fun than it had been the year before. Gloria took Malcolm and me to town and told us we were getting a stocking for Lexi. I had mentioned that Spark had his own Christmas stocking, and Malcolm had bugged his mom to let us get Lexi one. We were going to surprise Gabe—and Lexi. We found a great one—red with fur at the top and a dog that looked sort of like Lexi embroidered on the front. We got some dog biscuits and a squeaky toy to fill it.

"Lexi'll love this!" Malcolm exclaimed.

"I'm sure she will," said Gloria. "And so will your dad." There was a tone in her voice that seemed really caring. I knew that Gloria still wasn't too sure about how she felt about Lexi. She still acted a bit stiff around Gabe's dog, but for Gabe's sake, it seems she was trying to get used to Lexi. Malcolm told me later he was surprised her mom had gotten the stocking for Lexi.

"She never had dogs growing up," he told me. "I think she's not quite sure how to act toward them. And then knowing that Lexi is Dad's dog confuses her even more. But she sees that Dad is a lot happier since Lexi's arrival. He's not as grouchy, and he doesn't forget things as much. Lexi is great with my little sisters, and they love her. So I guess Mom believes that Lexi is a good thing—I think. Maybe getting her a stocking means she's trying to say that Lexi is part of the family and Mom's glad."

"How can you not love a dog?" I asked, remembering when Spark came to our house.

"Spark has so much personality, and he makes us laugh a lot. Like when my mom folds wash and he hands her the socks or underwear out of the laundry basket at her feet. Sometimes he's in such a hurry to get a pair of pants, he'll get his head into them and looks so funny. And he loves to find the dryer sheets and looks so excited when he can give her one."

Malcolm laughed. "Lexi's pretty funny, too. I hope Mom's coming around. At least she hasn't threatened to leave lately."

I knew that was always on Malcolm's mind—the fear that his mom would leave and take his sisters to live with her. He didn't want that even if his sisters could be real pains sometimes.

Christmas was really fun. It snowed on Christmas Eve but fortunately not until we got home from Christmas Eve service at the church. Waking up to snow on Christmas morning made it really great.

We let Spark out in the back yard as soon as we got up, and he danced around and threw snow over himself like he always did. He loved water in any form, even frozen. Mom called him back in, and we went into the living room to open our stockings.

I loved seeing the Christmas tree all lit up. Spark got a squeaky toy in his stocking and he had a great time bringing it to Mom or me to throw for him. We had to make sure to throw it away from that tree so he wouldn't knock the ornaments off with his wagging tail. When he was home without his service dog vest and not on duty, he was just a crazy ole dog.

Aunt June and Uncle Bob came over for presents and to help make breakfast. I loved our Christmases together. Later in the day, we were invited to the Davises' for dinner. They planned to go to Florida to visit Gloria's parents over the New Year holiday but wanted to be in their own home for their first Christmas there.

Lexi and Spark seemed as happy to get together as we all were. Lexi guarded her new toy at first but finally allowed Spark to play with it, too.

"Thanks for helping Malcolm with Lexi's stocking," Gabe said to me. "She loves it, and I do, too," I saw him smile at Gloria. I think she had told him all about our trip to find the stocking.

"I'm excited about seeing my grandparents," Malcolm told me after dinner. "But Lexi's going, and they don't like dogs. They didn't want Dad to bring her, but he said that not taking her was out of the question. Mom and he had a fight about it. First one they've had in a while. If Lexi stayed home, so would he, Dad told Mom. Mom's worried about taking a dog on the plane, too."

"These dogs are fine on planes," I told him. "We took Spark to California once. He just curled up and went to sleep. You have to tell the airline you have a service dog though."

"Yeah, ABL told us to do that, and we did. I just hope it all works out."

So did I for Malcolm and his family's sake.

Lexi's Alarm

It was lonely without Malcolm for the rest of Christmas vacation. Mom kept going to the vet center, so I went with her, but it was too cold to sit by the pond. I sat in the van and listened to music. I was glad when Malcolm got back and we started school again. But Malcolm seemed kind of glum.

"How did it go?" I asked him. "Did Lexi like the plane ride?"

"She did great," he told me. "Just like you said, she slept all the way." He still didn't look that happy.

"So what went wrong?"

"My grandparents just didn't get it. They worried that Lexi would get on the furniture—she doesn't unless she's asked. And when we went out, they asked did we have to take 'the dog' like she was a real pain. I don't think Dad enjoyed it at all. And on the way back, Mom didn't look too happy, either. They've been fighting again."

I had no idea what to say to Malcolm. I guess not everyone understood how a service dog could improve life. Evidently for some people, a dog was no improvement.

The rest of January was pretty cold and icy, so we didn't get too many walks in together. Malcolm came over, and we played with a couple of the new games he had gotten, but he didn't seem happy. I tried to cheer him up by clowning around and having Spark show him something new we had taught him. We'd put a small Frisbee on his nose, and when we told him to, he'd flip it into the air and catch it. I thought it was really funny, but it didn't seem to cheer up Malcolm.

At school, it was time for class projects. Each year we would do a project and then present what we had done at a big fair at the beginning of March. Each project had its own table, and people walked around and looked at the projects. I asked Malcolm if he wanted to go in together and do something on service dogs and what they can do. He didn't seem that enthused about doing it, but finally he agreed. When I got home, I told Mom about our project and asked if she'd take us to ABL some time so we could find out more about service dogs.

"Sure," she answered. "I'll call them. Maybe they'll give you a tour."

Great, I thought. This will be a super project. Mom arranged for Malcolm and me to go to ABL one day during February vacation. I had looked up a lot of stuff on the Internet, but I wanted to talk to someone because I had lots of questions.

The Saturday after we got out for vacation was cold and cloudy. Gloria had taken Malcolm and his sisters to their dentist appointments. Otherwise I might have asked if Malcolm could come over.

"Come on. Let's take Spark for a walk," Mom said as she hooked on his leash. We had an ice storm a couple of days before, and there were still patches of ice. We planned to be careful.

"How's the project coming?" Mom asked as we headed out for our walk. "Are you looking forward to our appointment at ABL this Thursday?"

"Good, I guess. We have a lot of information and are starting to think about the poster we'll have at our booth, but . . . "

"But what?" Mom stopped looking concerned.

"Malcolm doesn't seem that into it."

Mom was quiet for a minute as we walked along.

"Malcolm may be having a tough time at home, Sunny," She explained quietly. "Gloria isn't sure that Lexi was a good idea, and Gabe is convinced that the dog is good for him. I think it's been kind of rough for everyone."

"They're not going to move out are they?" I asked, echoing Malcolm's greatest fear.

"I really don't know."

It was then that Spark stopped short. He perked up his ears as if listening for something. Mom stopped and looked at her dog. It was so unlike him to just stop short.

"What is it, Boy?"

Spark sniffed the air and began to whine. Then he barked urgently. Looking at Mom as if trying to figure out what to do, he barked again and started off down the street. Then he stopped, looking at Mom and barked. It was so unlike his usual behavior.

"Let's go, Spark," Mom finally said and let him head in the direction he wanted. It was not long before we heard what Spark's sharp ears had heard before us—another dog barking.

"Is that Lexi?" we asked almost together. After hearing her yip and play with Spark so often, we easily recognized her bark.

As we hurried down several streets and around a corner, we saw Lexi standing over something and barking insistently.

"Gabe!" Mom recognized the situation immediately. Gabe lay on the ground apparently unconscious as Lexi barked her alarm. Just then, the door of a nearby house opened. A man emerged, obviously annoyed.

"What is all this racket . . . " he began and stopped short when he saw Gabe on the ground. Then he spied Lexi's service dog vest. I leaned over my friend's dad and saw that he was bleeding.

"Mom, he's hurt!"

"Edna, call 911!" the man yelled back into his house as he rushed over to us.

"What happened?" he asked.

"We don't know." Mom answered breathlessly. "I guess he slipped on ice," she added, pointing to the patch of ice on the sidewalk.

"Lucky we heard this dog," the man said as he knelt beside Gabe to check him out. "He could have frozen out here."

Lexi apparently concluded she had done her job in summoning help and quieted. Still, she seemed obviously nervous. Whimpering softly, she sat beside Gabe.

"It's okay, girl," I said as I patted her gently. "You did good work."

"Hey, Deb! Come out here, quick," the man yelled into his house. And then to us he said: "My wife's friend's an EMT. She just stopped by on the way home from her shift."

A young woman still dressed in her EMT uniform came out of the house and bent down to look Gabe over.

"It looks like he hit his head." The EMT pointed to blood on Gabe's scalp. "This weather can be treacherous for someone on metal crutches. Good thing he has this dog." Her friend petted Lexi appreciatively.

"And good thing we have you," I heard Mom say as she stroked Spark with thanks for his part in the rescue. Another woman emerged from the house with a blanket. The EMT covered Gabe who was just beginning to come to.

"Lexi," he murmured. "Where's my dog?"

"Right here," the EMT told him, "and good thing, too. Now try not to move too much. Help is on the way." We could hear a siren in the distance.

"Did you slip on the ice?" the woman who brought the blanket asked while the EMT knelt by Gabe determining if there were other injuries.

"No," Gabe said weakly. "My leg just collapsed. It's been getting worse . . . "

An ambulance rounded the corner and came to a hasty stop at the curb. Two EMTs jumped out.

"Hey, Deb," one called, obviously recognizing their fellow EMT examining Gabe. "What's up?"

The two men talked with Deb, and they soon had Gabe bundled on a stretcher and into the ambulance.

"My dog!" Gabe said urgently as they put him into the ambulance. "I want Lexi!"

"A service dog?" the EMT asked before she saw Lexi's ABL vest. "Okay. Come on, Pup." Lexi jumped into the ambulance with Gabe.

"Darn nice looking dog," one of the other EMTs murmured almost under his breath.

As they closed the doors. Gloria's SUV came around the corner on the way home. Malcolm and his sisters were with her. They saw Mom and me and the ambulance and screeched the car to a halt.

"What happened?" she called out of the window. She was obviously concerned.

"Gabe fell," Mom told her. "Lexi alerted us. They are taking him to the hospital to see if he's okay."

Gloria got out of the SUV looking worriedly toward the ambulance.

"Mommy!" Sherry called from the SUV. "Where's Daddy?" Both girls had started to cry as they realized something was wrong.

"Stay there girls. It'll be okay," Gloria said as she moved toward the ambulance. Seeing the man from the house she said, "Where are they taking him? He's my husband."

The man came closer to her.

"You're his wife?" When Gloria nodded, her eyes filled with tears, the man continued.

"Probably just hit his head. I think he'll be fine, but we wanted to be sure. You can meet them at the hospital—St. John's." He told her. And then: "Good thing he had that dog, or he might still be lying here in the cold."

Tears streaming down her face, Gloria started to put her car in gear, evidently to head to the hospital.

"Gloria, wait!" Mom called. "Let me take the kids."

Gloria said something to Malcolm and his sisters, and they piled out of the SUV. Joy clung to her mother, who was trying to explain to her.

"Joy and Sherry, go with Malcolm. Amanda will take you to her house. I need to go to the hospital with Daddy. The man said he will probably be okay, but I need to go with them and talk to the doctors. Be brave, girls, now, and go with Amanda."

To Malcolm she said, "Take good care of your sisters. I'll let you all know what is happening."

"Thanks. I'll call you," she said to Mom and drove off hurriedly along the route that the ambulance had taken.

"Come on, guys!" Mom said to all of us. "Your dad's getting help. Let's go back to our house and have some hot cocoa!"

Malcolm and I glanced at each other. Mom was obviously trying to make us all feel a bit better, especially the little girls. Maybe she thought cocoa would take their mind off their dad being taken to the hospital, but I doubted it. "He'll be fine," I told Malcolm. I hoped it was true and wished there was something I could do. I felt so helpless.

Malcolm nodded but did not say anything. By this time both Sherry and Joy were crying and asking him all kinds of questions. Although he looked close to tears too, he gave them a weak smile.

"Come on, you guys. I want some cocoa. Let's go!"

Back at our house, Mom and I made cocoa while Malcolm tried to comfort his sisters. He was upset, too, but trying to be like an adult and not show it. Mom put on a Disney movie for the girls, and we watched it, too, just to keep our minds occupied.

Later, as we made supper for everyone, Gloria called. Gabe had a slight concussion from hitting his head, and the doctors wanted to keep him at the hospital overnight to be sure nothing was too serious.

"Let the kids stay here overnight," Mom offered. "You can stay there with Gabe if you want."

I was surprised when Gloria agreed, as she was quite protective of the girls and Malcolm. But I guess she knew they were safe with Mom and me. She knew she wanted to be with Gabe.

We started to play Uno, a card game that even little Joy loved, but it was clear that Sherry and Joy were tired. Mom found some t-shirts that were much too big for them but still made good night-gowns. We piled the two of them into the guest bed, and Malcolm and I read them a story. We tried to make it like a pajama party, but the little girls were pretty quiet.

"Hey, look," Malcolm whispered. Sherry and Joy were fast asleep, curled up together on the big bed. I hadn't even gotten to the third page of the book.

"Come on, you two," Mom said when we came back into the living room. "I think we should all get some sleep. We don't know what tomorrow will bring. Maybe we can see your dad, Malcolm." Malcolm offered to sleep on the couch, but I gave him my room and slept with Mom in her big king-sized bed. I don't think anyone slept a lot, but at least we knew that Gabe would be okay.

And we had Lexi and Spark to thank.

More News

Mom and I just finished up our pancakes the next morning when Gloria arrived. I was surprised that she had Lexi with her. I figured Gabe would want to keep Lexi.

Gloria looked worried. I figured something must be wrong: maybe Gabe wasn't okay. Mom and Malcolm saw Gloria's worried look, too.

"Is Dad okay?" Malcolm asked.

"Yes . . . and no," Gloria began as she unhooked Lexi, who immediately greeted Spark. The dogs seemed glad to see each other.

Malcolm and his sisters gathered around their mom.

"What is it?" my mom asked. We were all thinking the same thing.

"His head is fine," Gloria began. "He didn't even need stitches even though his head wound bled a lot like many do. But they found something about his leg, and they don't like it. The doctor wants to operate. They don't want him on it. They'll keep him for another day to make sure he's okay for an operation."

Joy, the littlest of Malcolm's sisters, began to cry and ran to her mother, who hugged her. Then Gloria and the little girl were both crying. Sherry rushed to her mom, and the three of them hugged and comforted each other.

"Will Dad be okay?" Malcolm asked in almost a whisper.

"The doctor thinks this will actually help Dad," Gloria told Malcolm. "The pain has been getting worse," she said to all of us. "I was so worried. Gabe doesn't like to worry us, so he never really said much, but I knew that he was in a lot of pain."

"I could tell, too," said Malcolm quietly. Gloria gazed at her son and invited him into the family hug.

Malcolm went to them and hugged his sisters and mom. When he looked at me, I think he was a little bit embarrassed.

Mom smiled at me and offered me a hug, too. Then she said, "Why don't you take out the leftover pancake batter and make Gloria some pancakes. She looks like she could use some."

"That's okay, I . . . " Gloria started but then realized that my mom was giving her an opportunity to share more of what would happen while the little girls were not in the room.

As Malcolm and I started to take Joy and Sherry back into the kitchen, I noticed Lexi go over to nuzzle Gloria, who stroked her gently. It was the first time I had seen her do that.

"Yes, Lexi girl," said Gloria softly. "We owe you a lot. Thanks for saving my Gabe." Malcolm and I paused in the doorway exchanging a look. Had something changed?

"Lexi will be a big help when Gabe gets home," Gloria told Mom. "He'll need to be in a wheelchair for a while he gets stronger. But you're up to it, aren't you girl?"

Mom and I exchanged looks. It seemed that Lexi had finally won Gloria over.

"The hospital says I can bring Lexi to visit and stay with Gabe for short periods. When he is out of surgery, he'll have to go to a rehabilitation center, and she can stay with him if we're willing to come over and take her out until he gets mobile," Gloria explained.

"We can help," Mom assured her. "I can go over sometimes, and Sunny and Malcolm can go with me when they get out of school. We'll work it out."

Hearing some dishes rattle in the kitchen, Malcolm and I hurried out to see what the girls were up to. We smiled at each other. Things were working out. In the meantime, Joy and Sherry had leftover pancake batter out of the fridge and were getting ready to ladle it into a fry pan as they had seen Mom do earlier. We were just in time to keep them from making a big mess.

After Gloria and the kids left to go home, Mom told me what they had discussed. Gloria planned to take some time off from work to be with Gabe while he was in the hospital and rehab, but if we helped, it would make it a lot easier for the family. Lexi could be with him once he went to rehab, but the regulations at the rehab center did not allow them to take Lexi out or care for her.

We arranged that we would take turns going to the rehab center to take Lexi out until Gabe was able to do so as part of his physical therapy. Gloria would be there a lot of the time, but she also needed to spend time with the kids. Mom and Malcolm and I were going to keep Sherry and Joy amused while Gloria was with Gabe. Then we would take them in to visit and they would go home with Gloria for awhile while Mom and I helped with Lexi. We jokingly said that we would be The Lexi Brigade.

Gabe had his operation on Tuesday and came through it well. Gloria told Mom that the doctors had repaired more of his injury and put a rod in his leg so that he would be able to walk again with his crutches if all went well. But that would take time and physical therapy. For now, he was using a wheelchair just like Mom. The doctor had told Gloria that Gabe would probably move to rehab in a few days or next week.

Mom said we could go in to see Gabe on Wednesday afternoon. Gloria was just rushing the kids out to get them home when we arrived. "Hey," Malcolm greeted me. "I'll call you later."

"Great," I said and watched them go off.

Gabe looked pretty tired so Mom said we wouldn't stay too long. He was sitting up in bed but there was a wheel chair next to the bed.

"Guess I'll be in this thing for awhile," he said indicating the wheelchair.

"You get used to it," Mom smiled at him. "And with physical therapy, it sounds like you'll be up and around again soon."

"I'll still need the crutches but they say that it shouldn't hurt as much to walk."

Mom and Gabe talked for a bit. I wasn't really listening as there was a ballgame on the TV, until I heard Mom say, "Come on, Sunny. Let's let Gabe get some rest." And then to Gabe, "Get some rest here. Once they get you into rehab, they'll work you pretty hard."

Gabe smiled weakly. " Don't I know that! Thanks for coming in. See you soon."

"He's coming along," Mom said cheerfully as we walked out of the hospital and found our van. It was cold and it looked like it might snow again. I think Mom was anxious to get home. I wondered how she felt knowing that Gabe would walk again.

"How come they couldn't have done something so you could walk?" I asked Mom on the way home. She looked a little sad, and I wondered if I shouldn't have asked the question. But Mom was pretty open in talking with me about her injuries now that I was older.

"Because it is my spine that was damaged. Remember I told you that?" Mom explained, and I nodded. I did remember, and I was glad she didn't seem to mind talking about it.

"Everyone's injury is different," she continued. "I'm just glad that Gabe has a chance to walk again. And I'm doing okay," she told me. "Especially with the help of my Sunny!"

I felt all warm inside hearing that.

On Thursday, Gabe was still in the hospital and Gloria had taken Sherry and Joy in to see him while Mom took Malcolm and me to ABL to get more material for our project. Marge and the other people who worked there said hi to Mom. I had met some of them and they all seemed really nice.

"We were sorry to hear about Gabe's fall and his operation," Marge told Mom. "But," she continued "We are also glad that Lexi saved the day."

"These dogs are pretty special!" laughed Mom as she petted Spark, who sniffed the air, probably remembering the smells of his life at ABL.

Marge showed us around. We saw where the dogs stayed after they came in for their final training and even the training room, a very large room with plenty of space for dogs and their partners to go through training tasks.

"Hey, this is where your mom and my dad trained with their dogs," Malcolm said. Spark seemed to remember, too, as he looked up at Mom as if waiting for some command.

Marge laughed. "I think he remembers playing, too," she commented. "We take off the dogs' vests and let them play up here especially when the weather is bad. Feel free to give him some exercise, Amanda. There are some throw toys here that you can have him fetch. In this weather, take advantage of this indoor exercise opportunity. I'll take the kids around and give them some pamphlets and things. You've seen the place anyway."

"Sounds good to me," said Mom as she called Spark to her. She took off his vest. Marge handed her a toy, and Mom threw it. Spark retrieved it and seemed happy. He reminded me of a puppy as he ran and got the toy. I'm sure Spark recognized this as play time.

"Come on, kids," said Marge, "I'll show you the rooms that your mom and dad stayed in while they were here for training."

Marge took us to another building with separate single bedrooms and a common kitchen and sitting area.

"This was your mom and Spark's room," Marge said, showing us a pretty room with a bed and decorated with cool dog pictures on the walls. Like all the other rooms there was also a large dog bed in one corner for the room's canine occupant.

"And your dad and Lexi were here," Marge told Malcolm as she showed us a room just like Mom and Spark's.

"Are all the people who come here veterans?" Malcolm asked.

"No, we have lots of other folks who need service dogs. People have all different types of needs. We even train dogs to help people who cannot hear."

"Really? What do the dogs do?"

"Well, they alert their owners to the phone ringing or the doorbell. They even wake them up when the alarm clock goes off."

"Wow, I never thought about not being able to hear things like that," said Malcolm.

"One lady came to us for a dog because she realized that she couldn't hear her baby cry. That's how babies communicate to let their parents know that they need something," explained Marge.

"So the dog helped her to hear that the baby was crying?" asked Malcolm.

"The dog told her that the baby was crying. That new mom's story had a lot of the staff in tears," Marge commented.

I had learned some of the answers to Malcolm's questions over the time we had Spark, although the story of the mom and her baby was new to me. My mom sometimes volunteered to help ABL when they had a booth at a local event like a fair. So she had learned all about the services they offered. But I liked the fact that Malcolm was asking questions. He was really getting interested in our project.

"These rooms are great," said Malcolm as we saw one more client room. "Like a hotel!"

"But very dog friendly!" Marge laughed. "Come on, let's go to my office, and I'll give you some materials for your display."

At her office, Marge gave us pamphlets and brochures about ABL. They had pictures of dogs doing various things for their people.

"And since you are going to do such a good job with this presentation," Marge said, I'll give you this. She handed Malcolm and me a DVD. "Why don't you watch it while I tell your Mom that we are almost finished and to meet us in the lobby." She took the DVD from its sleeve, turned on the DVD player she had in her office, inserted the disk and pushed play. Malcolm and I sat back to watch.

The narrated DVD was pretty short and talked about all that service dogs can do for people, giving some demonstrations with real people and dogs.

"People will love this!" I said.

"Yeah. I'll ask Dad if I can bring in his laptop to show it on. He lets me use it sometimes."

After we watched the DVD, Marge returned, gave us our own copy of the DVD, and went with us to meet Mom in the lobby. Spark was panting. He had enjoyed playing hard, I guess.

"Thanks so much, Marge," we said almost in unison.

"You are very welcome. Anytime," Marge responded. "Oh, and take pictures and let me know how it goes."

"Wow! This is great stuff," Malcolm said as we rode home from the ABL center. "This will be a super project!" From the questions he asked the ABL staff, I decided he was really excited about the project.

Spark seemed to enjoy being back at ABL, too, but when it was time to leave, he was eager to go with Mom.

A week later Gabe was transferred to the rehab center, and we began our trips to take Lexi out. I was glad that it was only a few blocks from our house. We could have walked, but Mom usually drove us, especially since we were taking little Sherry and Joy and it was too far for them to walk.

When we got to Gabe's room, Lexi greeted us happily, especially Spark, but also seemed happy to return to Gabe after we took her for her walk. The staff at the rehab center became fond of her and loved having her around. Gabe seemed happy, too, and told us the physical therapist helping him would soon be using walks with Lexi as part of his therapy.

One day, Malcolm, Mom, and I talked with Gabe after taking Lexi out. A nurse wheeled a man into the room and helped him into the next bed.

"You're back!" Gabe greeted him enthusiastically.

"Boy, they sure work you hard in physical therapy here," the man said, obviously tired.

"Meet my new roommate, Ron," Gabe introduced him to all of us. "We've been talking and figured out we were in Iraq at the same time."

"And I've been admiring this beautiful dog," Ron said, indicating Lexi. "I should get a helper like this."

"And I got Lexi after meeting Spark," Gabe explained. Hearing his name, Spark lifted his head.

"Another one! Wow," said Ron. "Helper dogs come in all colors." He laughed. I was all ready to tell him to call ABL when I saw Mom's look at me. I remembered then what she had told me, that service dogs weren't for everyone and you had to wait until someone was really serious about getting one.

I loved our dogs, and I could not imagine why everyone wouldn't want one.

The Project Fair

It was almost March and the day of the Project Fair. Malcolm and I had worked hard on our poster and exhibit in between helping Mom and Gloria with Lexi and all our other homework and chores. Gloria had returned to the lawyer's office part time, and Gabe's physical therapy included some walks with Lexi. Mom, Malcolm and I were able to cover the times when Gabe couldn't take her out or Gloria was at work.

"I really wish we could take Lexi out," one of the nursing assistants told us. "But the rules say that any service animal is the responsibility of the patient. Lexi is such a patient dog, though. And so pretty."

Malcolm and I loved helping Gabe with Lexi and doing so made us even more anxious for the Project Fair.

When the day of the Project Fair arrived, we set up our table with the others in the school cafeteria. The fair doors would open after school from three to five, when people could walk through and see our projects.

Gloria took time off from work to do Lexi duty that day and come to the fair. Mom was there so we could demonstrate some of the things Spark does for her.

We had a great time telling people all about service dogs, and Malcolm even shared how Lexi and Spark had saved his dad. People loved our exhibit.

"I wish Dad could be here," Malcolm said.

"He'd be really proud of you," Mom told him.

At five, we knew the winners would be announced. We waited expectantly as Mr. Barrett, our principal, went to the microphone. He thanked every one for coming and then announced:

"The third prize goes to Joshua Dowe and his exhibit on robots." Everyone clapped as Joshua went up to get his prize a plaque with his name on it and twenty dollars in cash. "The second prize goes to Taylor and Madison Russo for their project on motion and how our muscles help us move." More applause while they got their plaques and money envelopes. I was glad that my two friends had gotten the prize. They worked hard on their project, too.

"And now, ladies and gentlemen, boys and girls, I am proud to award our first prize to two special young people who have not only learned a great deal about their subject but whose lives have changed for the better because of their subjects. The first place goes to Sunny Carter and Malcolm Davis for their project on service dogs."

As applause grew louder again, Malcolm and I proudly accepted our prizes. Mom had apparently told Spark to speak, because I could hear his enthusiastic bark above the noise.

"I just wish Dad was here," Malcolm murmured again as he went back to our booth and a beaming Mom, Gloria, Uncle Bob, and Aunt June. When the prizes had all been awarded and the presentations were over, Mom hugged us both.

"Congratulations, you two. And I have an idea. But wait. Aren't you supposed to pack up your stuff?"

"We can do it tomorrow," I said. "The teacher said we could do it after school tomorrow."

"Why wait?" Mom urged. "I have the van. Let's get everything now. And maybe we can get pizza and ice cream on the way home."

The adults helped us take down our exhibit, and we loaded it into Mom's van. They buzzed among themselves as they worked, probably figuring out who would come back to the house.

"We'll go on ahead," said Uncle Bob. "We'll meet you at the house. Come on girls," he said to Sherry and Joy. "Why don't you come with us."

They liked Uncle Bob and Aunt June and were eager to go with them.

Mom, Malcolm and I started off in her van with Gloria following in their SUV. "Before we get some dinner, I want to make one stop," Mom told us.

When she pulled into the rehab center, we were both surprised.

"Are we visiting Dad?" Malcolm asked. We pulled around to the back of the building, which was unusual.

"You kids wait here," Mom told us as she got herself out of the van before calling to Spark, who as usual gave her his leash. The dog eagerly followed her.

Gloria pulled up behind us in the SUV. Mom was back in a minute saying, "Come on. Get your project stuff."

Malcolm, Mom, Gloria, two people from the center, and I carried our stuff into the building. But instead of going to Gabe's room, the staff people led us to a recreation room with several tables set up with some chairs arranged to face the tables.

"Now set up your stuff here," Mom told us indicating the tables. "Just like at the fair." We were still puzzled, but we did as she asked.

"Okay, we're all set up," I told her. And a minute later, some staff members wheeled Gabe in. He sat in his special new wheelchair with Lexi by his side. His roommate, Ron, followed in his wheelchair along with other residents in wheelchairs and on crutches or using walkers or canes. Staff members helped them all to take places in front of our exhibit.

"Now," said Gabe, who was apparently in on the plan. "Please, tell us all about service dogs."

And, so we did. We had two special dogs to demonstrate what service dogs can do—Spark and Lexi. We also played the video on Gabe's laptop that he'd let Malcolm borrow and handed the pamphlets that we had left.

People had lots of questions like "Who is eligible for a service dog?" and "How long does it take to get one?" They loved our presentation. Some asked for the number of ABL thinking they might like to apply for a dog. One of those people was Ron.

As we packed up our exhibit for the second time that day, Uncle Bob and Aunt June arrived with pizzas, ice cream, and Sherry and Joy who had gone with them to get it.

After we'd moved our project off the tables and packed it up in the van, the staff rearranged the tables and chairs and brought in more so we all could sit and eat. People were so friendly and came up to ask us more questions or to ask Mom and Gabe if they could pet the dogs.

We had explained in our presentation that you should always ask before you pet a service dog, and people had listened. I had my favorite ice cream—

chocolate chip. There was vanilla, too. From the look of Joy, there was also chocolate ice cream. Her little face was covered in it. Malcolm said he'd rather concentrate on pizza.

We even let Lexi taste her first ice cream—vanilla, because chocolate is bad for dogs, and she loved it.

"I'm so glad that we're all together," said Gloria as our little group sat at a table and ate our ice cream. There were tears in her eyes. "And I am thankful that we have Lexi, too."

"Hmmm," said Gabe, "I never thought I'd hear that!" I saw Gabe turn and wink at Malcolm before he added, "And what happens when your folks come up this summer? Will Lexi need to get a hotel room?"

Malcolm and I held our breath, hoping that a fight was not brewing. I remembered Malcolm telling me how his grandparents just did not understand how important Lexi was to Gabe, but Gabe seemed to know that Lexi had won Gloria over.

"Not a problem," said Gloria confidently. "I have already told them that Lexi is an important part of our lives now, and that is just the way it is. *They* can get the hotel room if they'd prefer!"

Malcolm and I cheered, and Mom gave us a look warning us to remember where we were. Lexi and Spark probably just wondered if there was any more ice cream.

Author's Acknowledgments from
Cynthia Crosson

There are many whose efforts result in the successful completion of a book—not only those who work on the actual manuscript but also those responsible for inspiration as well as care and support of the author.

I owe my inspiration to Kathy Foreman, Sheila O'Brien, and the staff at NEADS who have taught me so much about service dogs.

And to my illustrator Carole Williams who is not only talented but patient and who suggested that we do a book about physically challenged veterans.

Thanks also to Brenna Bean who read the manuscript and gave me important information and insight.

And to my nine-year-old granddaughter, Ruby, who approved the manuscript.

And where would I be without my editor and friend, Marcia Gagliardi, who does such a great job pulling everything together and keeping me on task, and who is always there with words of support and encouragement?

Thank you all.

Illustrator's Acknowledgments from
Carole Williams

It has been my great pleasure to again work with Cynthia Crosson on her latest book.

Thanks go to Marcia Gagliardi at Haley's for her help and suggestions.

I have to admit that I find illustrating a book to be the most difficult form of artwork I have ever done.

I am thankful for my husband Robert, his patience, and for being my greatest advocate in all that I do.

Cynthia Crosson

Author's Biographical Note from Cynthia Crosson

I learned after writing my first children's book, *Only Daddy's Dog*, how much fun writing for children can be. And what could be better than explaining to children the incredible benefits of service dogs.

My experience with service dogs began in 2005 when I received my own small helper, Dandi, from NEADS, a service dog organization in Princeton, Massachusetts, that places specially trained dogs with people who have a variety of disabilities. After being asked to serve on the NEADS board of directors, I was invited to develop a program for veterans with combat related PTSD. A professional therapist who had worked for many years with PTSD, I found the task a great challenge. The Trauma Assistance Dog Program, now a regular offering of NEADS, gave birth to *Only Daddy's Dog* as a way of explaining to children how service dogs can help.

The talented illustrator of *Only Daddy's Dog*, Carole Williams, suggested this book, *Sunny and Malcolm*. We hope that it will be the beginning of a series about the service dog, Spark.

When I am not working with service dogs and writing about them, you will find me at my computer in my Massachusetts home writing books on child abuse and child welfare. It comes from being a retired college professor who just never runs out of words or the desire to teach.

You may also find me in the pulpit of the First Congregational Church in Whately, Massachusetts, where I serve as pastor.

And I consult with Assistance Dog International about using service dogs with PTSD.

Carole Williams

Illustrator's Biographical Note from
Carole Williams

Drawing and painting have been my lifelong hobby. Just about every day, I spend several hours doing artwork. My interests are many and varied. I like creating pet portraits rendered from photographs and mostly done in colored pencil or acrylics. I also like creating personalized walking canes made with wood found in the Adirondacks or from along our lakes shoreline. I design each cane with a person's history, interests, hobbies, or sayings. I strip the wood of bark and burn in the words. Most canes have small carvings or hand-painted sketches. Birds, animals, and scenes from the Adirondack area provide endless inspirations for drawing and painting. Time is all to short to accomplish it all.

Music adds to each day's activities when I am not making art, and I enjoy playing the organ.